REDEMPTION

A Journey from
Tragedy to Triumph

REDEMPTION
A Journey from Tragedy to Triumph

by

Lynda Vialet

Copyright © 2018 Lynda M. Vialet. All rights reserved.
Published by Lynda M. Vialet/TheVlaway
ISBN: 978-1-5457-5110-7

This book or any portion thereof may not be reproduced or used in any manner whatsoever without the express written permission of the publisher except for the use of brief quotations in a book review.

Quantity Purchases:
Companies, professional groups, clubs, and other organizations may qualify for special terms when ordering quantities of this title. For information, email info@ebooks2go.net, or call (847) 598-1150 ext. 4141.
www.ebooks2go.net

Printed in the United States of America.

This book is based on actual events. I have tried to recreate actions, locations, and conversations from my recollections of them. To maintain the anonymity of certain people, I have changed the names of individuals and places. I may have changed some identifying characteristics and details, such as physical attributes, occupations, and places of residence.

DEDICATION

Every ninety-eight seconds another person experiences sexual assault.

This book is dedicated to the #metoo movement and to all the brave women and men who have stood up and faced their attackers. *No one* deserves to be raped or to suffer sexual abuse of any kind.

If you or someone you know has ever been sexually attacked, abused, or assaulted, please tell someone. Report it, speak your truth, and don't ever let anyone take your voice and your power away from you.

Always remember that it is *not your fault*. It took me a very long time to be able to open up and talk about what happened to me. I would like to thank each and every one of you for reading my story.

National Sexual Assault Hotline: 1-800-656-4673.

RAINN (Rape, Abuse & Incest National Network) is the nation's largest antisexual violence organization: https://www.rainn.org.

Me Too movement: https://metoomvmt.org/.

CONTENTS

Acknowledgments .... *xi*

Introduction .... *xiii*

Part I: The Tragedy *1*
    Chapter 1 3
    Chapter 2 8
    Chapter 3 13
    Chapter 4 19
    Chapter 5 23
    Chapter 6 27
    Chapter 7 31
    Chapter 8 36
    Chapter 9 40

Part II: The Trial *43*
    Chapter 10 45
    Chapter 11 50
    Chapter 12 54

Part III: The Triumph *59*
    Chapter 13 61
    Chapter 14 66
    Chapter 15 71

Epilogue *77*

References *79*

About the Author *81*

ACKNOWLEDGMENTS

This book is devoted to my amazing children and grandson—Anthony, Isaiah, and Mekhi—who are the reason that I breathe and continue to strive to be the best version of me. To my sister, who was always by my side for the happiest, scariest, and saddest moments in my life, and who is the wind beneath my wings. To my brother Luis, who is my rock and who always has my back 100,000 percent.

To my cousin Shannon, who supports me every step of my journey and is a huge part of my small village. She's my younger cousin, but she's who I look up to and who encourages me every day. To my cousin Charlene, who is always a huge supporter and has talked me off the ledge numerous of times. To all my BFFs, prayer warriors, and sister friends who pray for me and lift me up and guide me always to do my best and stay true to who I am.

To my precious angels in heaven who are watching from above: my parents, Cheryl and Rudolph; and my aunt Dee Dee. May they continue to rest eternally in peace.

A special thank-you to my aunt Tootsie for helping me along the way, and to my children's father, who ever since my mother took her last breath has supported and protected me and my children like no one else.

I love and thank each and every one of you from the bottom of my heart. You have all helped me to grow and to be strong and to fight against all obstacles to become the woman I am today.

INTRODUCTION

Trauma changes you; it physically alters your brain. Trauma changes biological responses within the human body. Trauma will affect every aspect of your life until you decide to take responsibility for your healing. There are eight billion people on this planet, and each person is different and has something unique and special about them. We share one common goal: we all share the need to be validated. When we endure tragedy, we find life's purpose through the pain. I believe this tragedy pushed me to find my purpose. We all have a story to tell, each and every one of us. This is *my* story.

PART I

THE TRAGEDY

CHAPTER 1

I was raised in a lovely section of South Jamaica, New York. The area was very culturally diverse. It was a community in every sense of the word; everyone looked after one another and cared about each other and the neighborhood. These were the times when you could be outside while your mom was in the house cooking or cleaning, and the neighbor would watch you. When you did something you weren't supposed to do, the neighbor could give you a smack on the behind, then bring you home, and you would get another one from your mom. I love that I grew up in that era. My earliest childhood memory is of my siblings and me riding on a sofa on the back of an old pickup truck, when we were moving into our new home. I was four years old. From the time I was born, we had lived with my maternal grandmother, so this would be our first home. It was as if I were asleep prior to this, and I was waking up and seeing the world for the very first time. The ride to the new house felt like an amazing adventure. The truck was loud and made a rumbling sound as we drove through the southeastern section of Queens.

My eyes were overcome by how enormous the sky was; I guess I never realized that before. It never ended. Every time we stopped, every turn we took, the sky just kept on coming along with us. It looked just like the ocean looks on television, clear blue and goes as far as the eyes can see.

All I could see were big white puffy clouds. It was so clear that it looked like I could just reach out and touch them.

Too young to know what I was feeling, watching my father and uncles load the truck felt the same way it felt the night before Christmas—when you feel excited because you know something good is about to come, but you don't know exactly what it is. Even at that young age, I knew that this was something to be excited about. Pulling up to the house, my little tummy was tumbling like clothes in a washing machine, and my legs were shaking like two little worms on the end of a fishing rod, I was so ready to jump out the back of that truck.

It was a small three-bedroom house with a basement and a nice, quaint front and backyard. It seemed huge to me. The floors were bare wooden planks, and they creaked as we ran across them. There were only three little ones running around, exploring the new house, but it sounded like a stampede going through the house as we ran around, up, and down the stairs, going in and out of each room. We were having so much fun exploring the new house. The walls had faux wood paneling on them, and right along the wall of the living room was this huge steel radiator—they don't even make those anymore.

Once we got settled in and met our neighbors, I felt a great sense of comfort and even as young as four years old, I knew right then and there that this was home. Over the course of many years of hosting barbeques and parties, our house soon became the place to be for the entire family and some neighbors too. My parents were the glue that held the whole family together. It seemed like we had parties every weekend, but it didn't have to be any type of celebration. It was always just the family getting together.

My father loved music, and every Friday he would buy whatever the newest R&B or Jazz album that was out, and he would play music. Both sides of my family were very close because they all grew up in the same neighborhood. In fact, one of my father's sisters married my mother's brother, so we spent a lot of time together. My aunts and uncles and cousins would come over, and we would all hang out and have fun, laughing and dancing and spending time together. Weekends filled with music, my mother's famous fried chicken and family were among the fondest memories I have growing up in that house.

When I was pregnant with my oldest son, all my siblings were still living at home. They all pampered me, which was really nice. My mom would cook any meal that I asked for, and my father would rub my belly and talk to it when he came home from work. My brother would go to the store for me and get whatever I wanted, and my sister would even polish my toenails for me because I couldn't reach them. Even after I had my son, they all had a hand in helping me raise him it was like a real village. That would always be home to me, even after I moved out.

So, when my father suddenly passed away in 1995, spending more time with my mother allowed me to build an even tighter bond with her. My brother Malik would pick my son up from day care, so I would go there every day after work to pick him up, and sometimes I would stay on the weekends. I was a single mom, so it was important to me that my son had stability so even though I moved to the other side of town, I still allowed him to stay over there sometimes, and I would go pick him up in the mornings and bring him to school from there. Being there felt like putting on an old pair of pajamas—it felt cozy and comfortable. My family always made me feel supported and protected. Although I had technically lived somewhere else, that was still my home. That was my neighborhood—where I grew up, where I developed my swag, where I always felt safe. Until one night, when all of that would change, and I would never feel the same about the neighborhood again.

It was a cold night in late November 1997, one of those nights that people should enjoy their sleep and wander deep into their dream worlds. I was about to leave my mother's house to walk home. It was only about a mile and a half away. I had done it so many times that it was nothing for me to even think twice about doing.

My son was asleep, he was six years old at the time. My mother was also asleep. I just wanted to get home to check on my place. I had been at my mother's house for the entire weekend, and that night I just wanted to sleep in my own bed. As I was leaving, I walked past my brother Malik, who was lying on the couch watching TV, and he stopped me. "Where you goin'?" he asked.

"I'm goin' home," I assuredly replied.

"You gonna walk?" he continued. "Why you gonna walk, you wanna take a cab, I'll pay for it." It was about two-thirty in the morning. I said, "No, I'm good," telling him I would be OK. It had always been OK. I had walked the same route at odd hours hundreds of times before. I looked back at him and walked out the door, disappearing into the early morning air.

CHAPTER

I was at a major turning point in my life. I was really struggling at that time. Nothing appeared to be going in the right direction—my life seemed as if it were falling apart. Being unemployed and not even being able to afford the basic luxury of a cell phone was really beginning to take a toll on me. I was on Section 8 and food stamps, and my mother was basically helping me to pay my bills and support my son. I did not want to become a burden in the first place, so I always felt uncomfortable about her doing so much for me.

Life has a way of humbling an individual's principles. It pushes you to one corner, and you feel as if cannot break free. You become extremely sensitive and selfless. I have always been independent, ever since I was a little girl and I never wanted to burden anyone with my troubles.

As I walked, I thought about where my life was going and what I was doing with myself, my twenty-eighth birthday was the very next week, and I was starting to get a little depressed. Long walks or rather walks, in general, have a way of allowing you to see a different perspective on things. Either they heal or compound some of your problems. It is like a self-evaluation exam.

As you walk, your legs drift into nothingness, and your mind wanders off into a state of either complexity or deep thinking. In my opinion, confusion is better than emptiness. At least you have variables to choose from; otherwise, you wouldn't be so confused.

It was cold. The old dark sky was perfectly clear, like a black piece of paper, and the air was eerily still. The tranquil, peaceful stillness of a midwinter snowfall was nowhere to be found. Rather, it was tense and uneasy, like the moment right before the killer jumps out of the woods in a horror movie. It wasn't the kind of stillness that lulls you to sleep. It was the kind of stillness that makes you conscious and alert.

Under the cover of darkness is where some of the worst crimes occur. All I could hear were the sound of my footsteps and the sound of me breathing. I walked down 116th Avenue to Lincoln Street, and then I walked up to Linden Boulevard toward the Van Wyck Expressway service road.

As I walked past the gas station, I saw a truck drive pass me real slow. It felt a little creepy because I could tell the man looked right at me, but I didn't pay it any mind because there were one or two other cars that went by me as well going in the opposite direction. I started walking down the service road, and I got a funny feeling. I could feel something wasn't right, so I turned around to look behind me.

I saw that same truck pull over and park, again I didn't really pay it any mind, but I did start to walk a little faster.

As I got closer to Lakewood Avenue, where I would turn the corner, I felt a weird presence behind me, the kind that raises the hair on the back of your neck. I could feel my whole body getting tense. I wondered later if that's the way a deer feels right before the wolf rushes in and carries it away.

Panic quickened my heart rate, and as I pulled my coat closer, I picked up the pace. Everything felt wrong, but it looked normal. Was I being ridiculous? I'd been walking these streets alone for years at all hours, and nothing bad had ever happened. Why would tonight be any different?

Just when I was about to take a deep breath and relax, something told me to turn around again. When I did, the wolf spoke.

He was a tall, light-skinned black man. He was big too. He was at least six foot, two inches tall. And he was heavyset—not fat but chunky. He chuckled with a nervous, panicky giggle, like a man who knew he had evil intentions. His eyes were unfriendly. They were fixated on me as he looked straight into my eyes.

He said, "Oh, I didn't mean to scare you, but I saw you walking, and I wanted to talk to you. Where you going? What's your name?" He started to get closer to me.

"Monica," I said, "and I'm going to my friend's house. She lives right here." I pointed to the house we stood in front of. I started inching closer to the house. It was dark inside, and there were no lights on at all. There were also no cars on the street; not one car passed us. It was quiet—a little too quiet.

The air was cold, but there was no breeze, no wind. It was as if time and the whole world stood still. My knees were shaking like my legs were made out of rubber bands. I felt like I was going to fall. I felt very nervous as I eyed my surroundings for an escape route.

I looked toward the other end of the street, but I knew the gas station was too far to run to, and the only thing next to us was the row of dark houses on one side and the entrance ramp onto the Van Wyck Expressway on the other. Either way, I was stuck. *This is not going to end well*, I thought to myself.

As he talked, he kept inching closer and closer to me. I kept backing up, trying to reach the stairs so I could run up and bang on the door of the house. He took a few steps closer to me. He was swaying, so I knew he was drunk. I smelled the strong stench of liquor on his breath, and I could see his eyes and his face very clearly now. That's a face I will never forget. His large round eyes were glaring at me, partly bloodshot but fully aware. He stared at me like a bull getting ready to burst through the gate, and I was dangling the red scarf.

He had a round face, and his chin was large, with a large mass of his upper neck underneath it. He was sweating even though it was cold outside.

He kept asking, "Where you goin'? Where you goin'? Why you out so late?"

I didn't say anything. I was too busy looking around to see how I was gonna get away from him. As he took more steps toward me, he backed me right up against the gate. It had a lock on it. I inhaled deeply; I knew I was in trouble. I looked out to the street, but again, all I saw was the entrance ramp to the massive three lanes of the Van Wyck Expressway.

I knew I didn't have anywhere to go, and before I knew it, he grabbed me and grunted, "no, you coming with me," as he yanked and dragged me closer.

I tried to scream, but before I could get the sound "n_" out, he put his large hands around my throat, squeezing so tightly that I could hardly breathe. He told me to shut up, and while he was choking me, he lifted me straight up off the ground like a rag doll.

With his massive hand around my throat and my legs flailing around, he carried me to his truck, which was parked at the other end of the street and threw me in the passenger seat. I was paralyzed with fear. I wanted to move, but I couldn't. With tears streaming down my face, gasping for air, it hit me that I was going to be killed. I thought to myself, *Oh my God, I'm gonna die*! Panic, fear, and shock hit me like a lightning bolt to the chest.

CHAPTER 3

It is a terrifying experience to be taken off the street and thrown into a truck without your consent. In fact, it is a life-shattering event. You begin to think you won't make it out alive. You're limited to two horrific outcomes: someone loses their life or gets hurt in the process. I loved my life, and I loved my son and my family, and I knew I was not ready to die that night. This kept recurring in my mind as the events of the early morning unfolded.

I was going to choose life over physical trauma. My mind started rambling, trying to think of ways to get out of this. What was I going to do? The future became blurry in a split second. When he got into the truck, he said, "I'm not gonna hurt you."

I started shuddering and crying, with my mind in a daze, thinking, *Did this really happen*? I was numb. I couldn't move. I could not believe this just happened to me. How could this be? I had walked that same route hundreds of times, and I was never afraid.

He was talking, but I couldn't hear what he was saying, because in my mind I was only thinking about what I needed to do to get out of that truck. There was a lingering reminder that whatever the case, I needed to act fast. I imagined everything I had to lose—all the precious things I had in my life. In this moment you forget about all the daunting things in life and focus on the positive things, the reasons you have to live.

A life-threatening tragedy is no different than a terminal illness. To some extent, you know death is inevitable, but hope keeps you alive. I imagined my six-year-old son at home, sleeping peacefully. My mother was sleeping when I left too. Nobody, but Malik even knew where I was going. They would simply think I was at home, and I did not have a cell phone to even call for help. *How am I going to get out of this? What is he going to do to me? Why is this happening to me? God help me please!*

As my mind drifted back to reality, I started to come terms with what was about to happen to me. I finally started to hear what he was saying. I heard him say in an aggressive tone, "I'm gonna ask you again: Where are you going?"

Panic-stricken and still trembling, I said, "I just wanna go home."

He snatched my pocketbook and dumped it out into his lap. Piece by piece he removed the items one at a time scanning each piece as if he was taking a picture of it with his mind's eye. He picked up my wallet and took out my ID. He read it out loud. A terror-stricken shock wave went straight through me as I listened to him read my whole name and my address, which was really my mother's address.

I was horrified. I didn't know what he was going to do to me, and I started shaking even more.

He put my ID on the dashboard, then he leaned across me and put my seat all the way back. He started driving.

As he drove away, he pushed my hat down over my eyes and told me to close my eyes. I could feel the scratchiness of his sweater, and I could smell the smoke, liquor, and sweat coming through his pores. The smell was so strong it made the hairs in my nose itch. My stomach was jumping and flipping like clothes tumbling in a washing machine. He told me to keep my eyes closed, but I was still able to see through my hat. He didn't know that, though.

As he drove around, I began to pray. I started to say The Lord's Prayer to myself, which was my grandmother's favorite, so I knew it by heart. I said it over and over and over:

> "Our Father, who art in heaven,
> hallowed be thy name.
> Thy Kingdom come,
> Thy will be done on earth,
> as it is in heaven.
> Give us this day our daily bread.
> And forgive us our trespasses,
> as we forgive those that trespass against us.
> And lead us not into temptation,
> but deliver us from evil.
> For thine is the kingdom, and
> the power, and the glory,
> forever and ever.
> Amen."

And you know what I realized in that moment? It's true—when you're faced with grave danger, you really do start to see flashbacks of your life. I began to think about how I didn't want to die at twenty-eight. I thought about my son and what his life would be like without a mother. I could hear the music my father used to play, and I could smell the fried chicken my mother would make every Friday. I started to think about my mother and how it would probably take her out of here if she had to learn her daughter was raped and murdered and found lying in a ditch somewhere. I thought about my son's smile and his laugh and attending his high school graduation and what he would be when he grew up. I thought about my father and how my sister and I used to stand on top of his feet, each one holding onto his leg and he would dance with us. I thought about my own childhood and how much fun I had growing up, spending time with my family.

He talked the entire time, but I couldn't hear a word he said. I was just crying and praying and crying and praying and crying and praying. *Where is he taking me? What is gonna happen to me? Lord, help me please. I can't fight this man. He's drunk, and he's twice my size. I don't even know where he's taking me.* I started crying even harder.

Finally, the truck stopped. I looked up, and I saw a familiar street sign: it was at the corner of 115th Avenue and 141st Street. He actually didn't drive too far, but it seemed like he drove a long distance. Every second felt like an hour. Although I knew I wasn't far from home, I still was very aware that this nightmare was far from over.

Once again, he told me, "You better not scream. I'm not gonna hurt you. I just wanna have sex, and I'll take you right back to where I picked you up."

I didn't say a word. I just sat there trembling for what seemed like ten minutes but was probably only about a minute. I wondered if he was thinking about how he was gonna kill me. Suddenly he leaned back and opened his pants. He shoved his hand inside them and took his penis out and started stroking it.

Looking straight out the front windshield, trying not to cry, trying not to shake, I could feel his eyes staring at me as if he were trying to get into my soul. A distressing feeling started welling up inside me. My stomach started doing flips. Out of the corner of my eye, I saw his hand start to reach toward me, and I cringed, thinking he was going to hit me. My heart started galloping at an increasingly rapid pace. Unexpectedly, I felt a hard yank on my coat, and then he told me to take my clothes off.

Still not speaking, I did what he told me to do. He grabbed my clothes and put them on the back seat; then he leaned over and roughly grabbed me by the back of my neck and pushed my head down into his crotch, forcing his penis into my mouth. I began crying again. I know he felt my tears, but he didn't stop. He started grunting and moaning, pressing my head up and down even harder. He grabbed me by the back of my neck again and pulled me up off him, then he pushed my head back down into the passenger seat. Before I could blink, he climbed across the armrest one leg at a time and got on top of me. He put his penis inside my vagina and started to have sex with me.

CHAPTER 4

I didn't move; I couldn't move. I didn't say a word. I just laid there. I could smell the sweat mixed with cheap cologne and alcohol on him. I started to feel dizzy, then he grabbed me by the hips and pulled me up and told me to get on top of him. Now he was more in control.

He grabbed my waist, digging his nails into my skin, wildly thrusting me up and down on top of him. He was groaning and sweating. "Tell me I'm the best you ever had!" he shouted.

I didn't say anything, so he dug his nails deeper into my side. I muttered it under my breath, and he finally ejaculated. He hauled me up and slid back into the driver's seat, breathing heavily. He reached across me into the glove compartment and grabbed some tissues to wipe himself off. He threw them out of the fogged-up window. Next he threw my clothes at me. Without even looking at me, and snarled, "Get dressed."

Getting dressed seemed to take an eternity. On normal occasions, getting dressed was an event for me. I would pose in the mirror and change outfits if something didn't look right. I would take pictures of myself with my digital camera way before they were called selfies. On this frightful day, getting dressed was a wish come true. It was assurance that this nightmare was ending, and I was going to live. The human mind has a difficult time processing danger. Being scared has a borderline; you are afraid until you aren't anymore, and that is very frightful to experience.

I fumbled and quickly got dressed. All the while this giant man was going through my things and putting my stuff back into my pocketbook; then he flung it at me. At that point he lifted my ID from the dashboard, and he roared my name out loud, this time my real name. "I thought you said your name was Monica. Why did you lie to me?" he growled with a frown on his face. I fumbled through some of my things, trying to play it off like I didn't know what he wanted. I finally mumbled yes and said my real name, looking down into my lap. He asked, "Why did you lie? You didn't have to lie to me. I told you I wasn't gonna hurt you."

The only thing running through my mind was the annoyance I was causing my captor. At this point I thought this was it. This was the moment he was going to kill me. I thought of how he could easily roll up my dead body after killing me. I thought about how it would be all over the news and how awful it would be for my family to live through such torment. I thought about my son and how he would never know that being his mom was the best thing I ever did in my life. I thought about how it would completely break my mother's heart, not even two years after she had lost my father.

Surprisingly, he handed my ID back to me and asked me where I wanted him to take me, so I told him to drive back down Linden Boulevard, and I would let him know where to turn.

As he drove, he started telling me that he liked me and wanted to see me again. The confusion and surprise hit me hard. Now I really feel like I'm in a dream. Did he really just say that? This man had committed a crime: he had just raped me. If there was one thing that I learned from all the crime dramas I'd watched, it was that lies save lives! I simply nodded in agreement. He turned up my block, and I dreadfully told him to stop; I could walk the rest of the way. I couldn't allow him to take me to the actual house.

Before I could get out of the truck, as if nothing happened, he asked how he could contact me again. I was at an impasse. I couldn't give him my mother's number. He dropped me up the street from her house. He knew the address, and I didn't have a phone at home or a cell phone, so I gave him the only other number I could think of—my sister's number.

I recited the number so fast I was surprised he even wrote it down correctly. I just wanted him gone. Giving him the number was the only way I could be certain I would get away from him. The situation felt awkward. I did not know how to react. In fact, I just stood there as he took down the number. After he wrote down the number, he repeated my name. I didn't even look back.

As he drove away, I started thinking to myself, *OK, I'm good. I'm safe. He didn't hurt me. He didn't kill me. It was just sex. I'm gonna go back in the house and take a shower and go to sleep and act like nothing ever happened.*

As I started walking, something was happening to me, I began shaking and shuddering even more. My mouth started watering. I was beginning to feel sick to my stomach, and my legs were getting weaker. By the time I reached the front door of the house, I was shaking so badly I couldn't even put the key in the doorknob, and my brother came and snatched the door open. I burst into tears. I fell into the door, landing on the floor, and I shrieked, "I just got raped!"

CHAPTER 5

I watch *Law and Order* all the time. I know what you're supposed to do when you get attacked. I know you're supposed to fight back, pull his hair, scratch your assailant, get his DNA under your fingernails, things like that. But when you are violated like that, there is nothing anyone can tell you about how you should feel or if what you did was right or wrong. One thing I've learned is that you never know what you're going to do when faced with danger until something happens to you. I had every intention of not saying anything, but as soon as I saw my brother Malik, I knew I had to tell. He woke his friend Darrin, who was lying on the other couch, and they ran out of the house so fast to see if they could catch him. But, of course, that guy was long gone. I was screaming hysterically, crying, shaking uncontrollably, and vomiting.

My mother called 911 first, then she called my sister Lorraine and my aunt Rose, who was a police officer at the time and worked at One Police Plaza. She met us at the hospital. Among other things, I felt so embarrassed, ashamed, and guilty, because I knew I didn't fight back. I didn't do anything to stop it from happening.

Rape is the only crime that attacks and criticizes the victim first. I knew everyone was going to look at me and judge me because I left the house that late. I wasn't dressed provocatively, and it was freezing cold that night. I had on a big coat, a scarf, and a hat. I also wore gloves and boots, but what was I doing out that late by myself? Why didn't I fight? Why didn't I scream? Why didn't I run? These questions haunted me for a very long time.

Lorraine rode with me in the ambulance. I was in shock the entire ride to General Hospital. It was like I had an out-of-body experience. I couldn't believe this really happened to me. I was inconsolable, hysterically crying and shaking the entire time. This was a nightmare I could not wake up from. The hospital was not very busy. It was cold and bright. I felt like everyone was staring at me and knew what had just happened to me. They put me in a private room way back in the corner, so I could feel calmer.

The hospital staff and the police treated me with so much respect, and I could tell they genuinely had compassion for me. The police questioned me and took my initial statement. They had to get all the details right away, while they were still fresh in my mind. I told them exactly what had happened, but I left out the part about giving him Lorraine's phone number. The guilt I felt was too overwhelming to share that in front of her.

I had to submit to a rape kit, and my sister had to leave the room. The nurse who administered the rape kit was very gentle. She explained everything to me step by step. First, she laid a white sheet on the floor and told me to stand over it and remove my clothes. Then she took pictures of me completely naked, front and back, she also took pictures of my face and neck in case there was any bruising. She took a swab of my mouth, vagina, and anus. She pulled hairs directly from the root from my head and from my pubic area. She scraped under my fingernails. She took blood and urine samples, and then a doctor came in and performed an internal vaginal exam.

They test you for everything—gonorrhea, chlamydia, syphilis, herpes, HIV, and pregnancy—and they give you medication for those sexually transmitted diseases in the event that you test positive for anything. They give you the HIV cocktail, a shot of penicillin, other antibiotics, and the abortion pill—the whole nine yards.

Going through that process makes you feel violated again, but I knew that it was necessary for the police investigation. Besides, I already told them what had happened, so I knew I had to be strong enough to go through it all the way to the end. I spoke to so many people that morning—police officers, doctors, nurses, and crisis counselors. I was physically and mentally exhausted by the time I got back to my mother's house. I just wanted to take a long hot shower and go to sleep.

When we got back to the house, my mother was still awake sitting on her bed. I could tell she was worried and had been crying. She asked was I OK, and I said, "Yeah." I could see the agony in her eyes. Aunt Rose told her the hospital took the rape kit and that when she got to work the next day, she was going to find out which detectives were going to handle the case and make sure they do a thorough investigation. We all were very tired, so Aunt Rose and Lorraine both went home.

I took that long hot shower that had been calling me all morning and went to lie down. It was about nine thirty in the morning, and my mother came in the room and handed me the phone.

"It's Lorraine," she said.

As soon as I said hello, I heard, "Do you know somebody named Tammy?" Lorraine said.

I said, "No. Why?"

She said, "Some girl named Tammy just called here for you."

"No, I don't know nobody named Tammy," I said, and we both hung up.

CHAPTER 6

Not ten minutes later, my mother called to tell me Lorraine was on the phone again. I took the phone, and Lorraine said, "Are you sure you don't know that girl Tammy? Because she just called again, and she gave me her number and said for you to call her."

I wrote the number down on a piece of paper, hung up, and called.

"Hello," she said.

"Yes, hello, can I speak to Tammy?"

"This is she," she said.

I said, "Oh, hello, my name is Lynda. You called me?"

"Yeah, do you know somebody named Biggs?" she said matter-of-factly.

"No, I don't know nobody named Biggs."

"Oh, OK, I must have the wrong number. Sorry." She hung up. It seemed weird for someone to be calling me right after what happened last night, but I didn't really think about it at all. I was so exhausted from everything that I just wanted to go to sleep.

"Oh, it's OK, no problem."

Two minutes later, Lorraine called me again. "Why is this girl Tammy calling you here?" she asked in a frustrated tone.

"I don't know. She asked me if I knew somebody named Biggs, and I told her I don't."

"Well, she called again, so you need to call her back and tell her to stop calling you here," she said, angrily.

"OK," I said. I called her back again.

"Hello?"

"Hello, Tammy?"

"Yeah, I'm sorry to keep calling, but are you sure you don't know anybody named Biggs?"

"No, I told you I don't know anybody named Biggs. Why do you keep calling me?" I started to get annoyed.

"I'm sorry, but did you go out last night? Are you sure you didn't meet somebody named Biggs?" she asked.

"Last night?" I asked. I'm thinking *I'm still trying to cope with the fact that I was choked, dragged off the street, and raped last night, let alone being poked and prodded and stuck with needles and questioned for hours, and I'm just now laying down, and you wanna know if I met somebody last night?*

"He's tall, light skinned. I'm sorry, but I found your number in my truck, and I know my husband went out, and I wanna know if you gave him your number," she said.

Now it hit me like a brick: I knew exactly who she was talking about. I started to shudder again. My heart started beating out of my chest. My hands were getting sweaty, and my stomach started doing flips.

I said, "Is he tall, light skinned, kind of heavyset, with curly hair? Does he drive a Jeep Cherokee truck with black on the bottom and burgundy at the top?"

"Yeah, that's *my* truck, and that's *my* husband, and I wanna know what's going on with yawl. I just found your number in my truck," she said straightforwardly.

I paused for a minute, then I said, trying not to scream and hold back the tremor in my voice, "Well, I don't know how to tell you this, but someone fitting that description, in that truck, raped me last night!"

"Oh my God! He did? Rape? Oh my God! I am so sorry! Are you OK? Oh my God! Did he hurt you?" she screamed.

"No, he didn't hurt me, but he did rape me," I replied.

"I'm so sorry." She just kept apologizing. She started talking, her voice was quivering, "We're married. We have a five-year-old son. We don't have any diseases. Well, I have lupus, but that's not a sexually transmitted disease." She paused and took a deep breath, then said, "I'm sorry to have to ask you this, but are you going to the police?"

I told her I had already gone to the police. I was in fact starting to feel pity for her. Why? I mean, I recognized the pain of being hurt by a man. I have been physically beaten, cheated on, lied to, manipulated, robbed, and now I had been raped. But to hear your husband has raped someone ... I don't know if I would've been able to handle that, so I felt genuine concern for her.

"I don't even know what to do. I don't know what else to say. Oh my God, I have to wake up his brother. They went out together last night. Can I call you back?" she said in a frenzied voice.

I kind of stuttered for a minute, then paused. I didn't respond.

"OK, I have to call you back." She hung up. She never called back.

I realized her anger was not directed toward me; it was out of fear. Her anger was prompted by the fact her husband could go to prison. Her fear was that she fell in love and married a man who could hurt other women. She wasn't concerned about me. She didn't even know me, and she didn't care that her husband had attacked me. All she cared about was whether or not I was going to go to the police. Nobody cared that I had been violated, except my family.

CHAPTER 7

Over the next few days, I went through a roller coaster of extreme emotions, from sadness to anger, fear, frustration, guilt, and anxiety. I was surrounded by family, but I still felt alone. I was trapped by my fear of being judged and ridiculed. It had consumed me and become very overwhelming. I felt trapped. I couldn't go home to be alone. I was experiencing panic attacks, flashbacks, and night sweats. So, I stayed at my mom's house, where I always felt safe. But being there, I felt like I was in a fishbowl. Everyone looked at me like I was fragile and going to break down at any moment.

I couldn't even look my sister in the eye. I felt an enormous amount of guilt and shame for what I thought I had done wrong. Every time the phone rang, I jumped. Every time there was a knock on the door, I jumped. I was a nervous wreck. I was torturing myself, but no one was blaming me but me. I was trying to be strong, but I couldn't take much more of it. So, when my cousin asked me to come visit her in Florida, I jumped at the chance to get away to a different place for a change in scenery and weather. I stayed at her house for about two weeks. It really gave me the time and the distance I needed to clear my mind.

My cousin Rhonda was a single mother of three who had experienced her own personal struggles. She was tremendously brave, and I had always looked up to her. Seeing her take on all her day-to-day responsibilities knowing what she had gone through, allowed me to find the confidence I needed to get through this tragedy and live a normal life.

The bus ride home gave me time to reflect on the two-week hiatus from my real life and focus on how I was going to move past this tragedy. When I went back home, I was determined to start the healing process, so I signed up for counseling and went to see a rape crisis therapist who helped me deal with the guilt shame and anxiety I was feeling.

I had weekly sessions for about a month and a half. In the beginning, I didn't really think I needed counseling, because I had my family to comfort and support me. I thought if I didn't think about it and got back to my normal routine, I would start to feel better, but once I started going every week, I learned that I really did need to talk to someone. I needed someone to help me understand why I was feeling the way I did.

Something was not right. I didn't feel like myself. I didn't realize the level of anxiety I was experiencing and speaking with a counselor helped me to cope with all the emotions I was dealing with. We didn't only talk about the rape. We talked about every aspect of my life: my son, being a single mom, my relationship with his father, my past romantic relationships, finances, and family, among many other things. We talked about diet and exercise, sleep habits, things that you would not normally think have any effect on your emotional stability. I learned that all of those are very important to the healing process, especially after being sexually attacked. Recovering from rape requires caring for your emotional and physical well-being. She also taught me that rape and abuse are the fault of the perpetrators, not their victims, even though they are often ridiculed by society.

I really needed to know that because the one thing I kept thinking about was how embarrassed I was because I exposed my sister by giving her number to my rapist. I was still experiencing a tremendous amount of guilt and humiliation. I didn't want people looking at me as if I were a victim.

You have to talk about it and let others know that it's OK to talk about it and that they're not alone. When you're violated like this, all you feel is loneliness. You feel like you're the only one going through it and that it's one way or another your fault. I shouldn't have given him my sister's number. I shouldn't have been out that late. I should have fought back or cried out for help, but I didn't.

For me, the critical part of healing was completely surrendering and understanding that what happened to me was not my fault. The crisis counselor helped me to finally accept that this was not the end for me. I was not a victim; I was a survivor. But I didn't feel like one.

Several weeks had passed, and I started to feel like I was slowly gaining control over my emotions. I wasn't feeling as nervous and anxious as I had from that dreadful morning. I noticed everyone was still looking at me like I was broken, and I didn't really like that feeling. I could see that everyone was concerned, and I felt protected, but I knew I had to go out into the world and face it head-on.

One evening, while we were all sitting around watching television, there was a knock at the door. Malik opened it, and there were two detectives from the Special Victim's Unit looking for me, a female detective and a male detective. Detective Garcia, the female, was tall, thin, and had really tanned skin. She looked like she was Italian. She was very fit, and she had really long, wavy hair. Her face was all made up, and she had a very nice smile. Detective Miller, the male, was an average-looking white guy—medium build, average height, and dark brown hair. We stepped into the kitchen, and they told me they were investigating my assault. They needed to ask me a few questions and asked if we could go down to the police station so I could make a formal statement.

I wanted my sister to go with me. She only lived about ten minutes away from my mother's house. My sister and I were only eleven months apart, so we were basically twins. We did everything together. It's like God gave me my very own best friend. My mother dressed us alike until we were around eleven or twelve years old. That's when we were able to pick out our own clothes. We had a love-hate relationship, but we were always taught you only have one sister. That's what our mother drilled into us. We fought hard, but we loved each other even harder. At the end of it all, we were always there for each other. I needed my sister, so they waited for her to arrive, and then we all left.

On our way to the station, the detectives wanted to go by the scene first to walk through it step by step. We drove along the same route that I walked. I pointed out to the detectives what I saw and where I saw him pass me. Although it was only about six o'clock in the evening, it was the middle of November, so it was already dark outside. To me, everything seemed to be moving in slow motion.

We pulled up to the house where the rapist stopped me, and we got out of the car. The detectives looked around as they took notes and pictures. It was still so surreal that I was literally standing in the same spot that a stranger picked me up, put me in his car, and raped me. It felt like I was watching a movie. I still couldn't believe that this really happened to me.

CHAPTER 8

The SVU is a special unit that handles sexual based assault crimes particularly. It was located in a regular-looking building off Queens Boulevard and 68th Avenue in Forest Hills. I probably passed that building over a thousand times in my lifetime, going up and down Queens Boulevard, and I had never noticed it. It felt so strange to be there after watching *Law and Order: SVU* so many times over the years. Detective Miller asked us if we wanted anything to drink—soda, coffee, or tea—and Detective Garcia took us into the investigation room.

The detectives gave me several books with pictures in them to see if I could pick him out. After a while everyone started to look alike. Besides, I knew he wasn't in there. His face was ingrained in the back of my mind's eye. I knew I would be able to tell instantly if I saw him. After all these years, I can still close my eyes and see his sweaty face. We went into this cold room with really poor lighting, and we sat at this long, cold metal desk. Detective Garcia did most of the talking. "What happened? Start from the beginning and don't leave anything out," she said. Both detectives had pads and were writing things down as I gave my statement. I was so worried because my sister was sitting right next to me, and I had to tell them in front of her that I gave my rapist her phone number.

Detective Garcia said that it was good that I did that because they had a way to track him down, and it should be easy to find and arrest him. I still felt guilty, though, because I didn't know what my sister was thinking. She didn't say anything, but the way she was looking at me I could tell she knew I was telling the truth. After I finished telling what happened, they told my sister to step out. They handed me a long yellow legal pad, and she asked me to write down everything that happened. So, I did.

About five days later, Detective Garcia called and told me that I needed to come down to the precinct because they had him in custody, and they needed me to identify him in a lineup. Subsequently, my sister and I went to the SVU unit once again. This time I was very nervous because I didn't know what to expect. I mean, you see these things every day on television, but you never expect to be actually going through it yourself. The whole experience had my anxiety level at an all-time high.

We got to the precinct, and this time my sister had to wait outside for me. This was the first time I met the Assistant District Attorney, Miriam Iqra. She was a very petite Jewish woman with a short pixie cut. Her hair was jet black, with a little bit of gray in it. She had pale skin and kind eyes. She introduced herself and told me she would be handling my case. She explained the lineup process and told me that I would be looking at five men. All I had to do was point out anyone I recognized. We went inside a room with a huge window that took up half the wall. The shade was down at first. It was dark in the room, but I could see the light on the other side of the glass. It was a two-way mirror.

In the room were myself, Detective Garcia, ADA Iqra, and another attorney, who I assumed was the rapist's lawyer. Detective Garcia pulled up the shade, and I saw all five men. I recognized him immediately. He was number four. I felt like I couldn't breathe, but I didn't say anything. I saw him looking all around the room with a stupid smirk on his face. "Do you recognize anyone? Take your time," Detective Garcia said.

"Yes, number four!" I replied.

The two lawyers started whispering to each other. I thought I had done something wrong, then Ms. Iqra said, "Can you point to the man you recognize and tell us how you recognize him?"

I pointed to him and said, "Number four—that's the guy who raped me." He was charged and arraigned in court that night.

After the initial arraignment, Ms. Iqra brought me into her office to tell me the status of the case. Over the next couple of days, I was exhausted and overwhelmed with meetings at the DA's office. I had to give my statement over and over and over again. We went over the strategy for the case and what she was going to need to do in order to get a conviction. She told me that the rapist had been ordered to give his DNA and that I also had to go to the medical examiner's office to give a blood sample so they could match the DNA.

It turned out the rapist's name was not Biggs. It was Frank Gray, and Mr. Gray was indeed married with a five-year-old son. He lived in Queens, not very far from where my mother lived, and he was a custodian at a school. The detectives were able to arrest him at his home because they tracked down his address by using the phone number his wife called me from. That was the good news. The bad news was that the case was weak.

There was very little physical evidence, no witnesses, and nothing that tied him to the case other than the phone number. He didn't physically harm me. They didn't have the results of the rape kit yet, which meant no DNA evidence, so first-degree rape would be very hard to pull off. Ms. Iqra asked me if I was OK with her charging him with sexual misconduct. It was a misdemeanor, but she would ask for the maximum sentence, which did require some jail time. The maximum sentence was one year.

That hit me like a wrecking ball to the stomach. I felt completely defeated after what I had endured, being grabbed and dragged off the street, and all they could charge him with was sexual misconduct? I felt humiliated and embarrassed. I felt violated all over again when I had to submit to the rape kit, and now she was telling me all they could charge him with was sexual misconduct? I just wanted to get over it and move on with my life. I agreed to go forward with the sexual misconduct charges. I definitely was not going to let him get away with what he did to me.

CHAPTER 9

I had just started to feel like myself again. I found a job with a temp agency and was working at Northside Hospital in the medical records department. It felt really good to have some sense of normalcy back in my life and to finally be able to better manage my finances. I rekindled an old relationship with an ex-boyfriend, and it started to feel as though my life was actually getting back to what it was before the rape.

I met Darius at General Hospital when Lorraine was giving birth to my niece. I was standing in the waiting area while the doctors checked on my sister. The security staff must have been changing shifts at that time because suddenly I saw about three hospital police officers come off the elevator and stand by the desk. All of a sudden, I heard one of the officers say, "I don't care. They all getting out of this hallway."

I looked up, and I thought to myself, *I know he's not talking to me. My sister is in there by herself, and I'm not leaving this hallway until her husband gets here.*

The next thing I heard was him escorting people out of the hallway and into the waiting room.

There weren't many seats in there, but there was a TV, a vending machine, and a huge window facing 165th Street. Some people went into the waiting room, some went to ask the nurse questions, and others went toward the elevator. I just stood there. Then I heard him say, "Excuse me, miss?"

I looked up at him. He was gorgeous. He was really tall, about six foot, four inches tall, caramel complexion, with a short, curly Afro, and he was gesturing toward me to come over to where he was standing. He said, "I would make you go in the waiting room too, but you're too cute, so you can stand here and talk to me."

I thought that line was corny but cute, so we both laughed. I introduced myself and told him I was waiting for my sister to give birth to my niece and that her husband had not arrived yet. I stood there with him for hours, and we talked until it was time for me to go in the delivery room because my sister was about to push. It was February 15, 1996, the day after Valentine's Day, and when I came back outside, Darius had given me a chocolate-covered cherry that he got from the store when he went out to lunch and said, "Happy belated Valentine's Day." I thought this was super sweet and romantic. We exchanged numbers, and he called me that same night when he got off from work.

We talked all the way through the next morning. We made plans for him to come hang out with me later that day. It must have been fate or destiny for us to be together because that night it started snowing and wound up turning into a huge blizzard, so he had to stay over. We were off and on for about a year, then we lost contact when he moved back to New Jersey. Darius had always been good to me, so when he called me out the blue, and I told him what had happened to me, he was very supportive and caring. We rekindled our relationship right from that moment.

It felt good to feel loved and cared for again. I wasn't alone at night anymore, and I was starting to regain my confidence. I was able to go outside without getting nervous each time a truck drove past me or when someone walked behind me. I was beginning to get back to my life the way it was before the rape, and it felt good.

PART

II

THE TRIAL

CHAPTER 10

Frank Gray was charged with sexual misconduct and was released on bail, along with a restraining order to stay away from me and to not contact me. Since I was the complaining witness, I was not able to go to each of the hearings. Ms. Iqra told me she would keep me updated with each step in the process, and she did.

Every time there was a hearing, or a motion made on my case, she would contact me and keep me up to date. She worked very diligently to get justice for me. She believed me, and that was so important to me. She said she would do whatever it took to get a conviction. I trusted her, and I believed her.

Over the course of the next several months, she called each time they went to a hearing. Each time court was convened, they would postpone it for another three to four months. Before I knew it, two years had passed, and I hadn't heard from Ms. Iqra in a long time, but I figured no news was good news. I fell right back into my old life. Lorraine and I had moved back home with our mom, and life was going really well for me. I was working at a bank in Long Island. I had my self-esteem back. I was hanging out at the clubs on the weekends and spending time with my son and my family during the week. Everything was back to the way it was supposed to be. I was genuinely happy again. I was dating, and I had not thought about the rape, Ms. Iqra, or Mr. Gray for a really long time.

In the summer of 1999, on a casual Friday evening sitting in my mother's living room watching TV, I saw a breaking news report flash on the screen. A Brooklyn man was arrested for serial rape. I felt my heart jump into my throat, and I looked up and saw him, the man who raped me, right there on the tv screen, and he was being led into the back of a police car with his hands cuffed behind his back.

When I looked at the TV, he was looking at the camera, and it looked as if he was staring right at me. I froze. I couldn't move. I couldn't breathe. It was as if time literally stopped right then and there. I jumped up from the couch, and I called for my mother. "Ma! That's him! That's the guy!" I yelled.

My mother saw the sheer terror on my face, and she didn't have to ask which guy. She knew exactly who I was talking about. "Are you sure?" she asked.

"Yes, I'm sure that's him," I said.

"Call the detective now!" she said.

I called Detective Garcia. She already knew what I was calling about, and she told me they had arrested him the night before. I had to speak with the DA's office on Monday, and they would let me know what I had to do next. I was on pins and needles for the entire rest of the weekend.

Once again, I went through the gauntlet of emotions—from being overwhelmed with joy, then back to being worried, then back to being happy. I felt nervous and anxious. I needed to know what was going to happen. *Serial rapist*, I thought. *If he raped someone else, now they have to bump the charges up for my case, right?* I felt vindicated already. People would finally believe that I was raped, not just sexually mistreated. That night I cried myself to sleep because I knew I was finally going to get justice for what happened to me.

I called Ms. Iqra's office on Monday morning at nine. She was already expecting my call. She told me to come into the office later on that afternoon, and she would explain everything to me and tell me what was going to happen next.

When a suspect submits a DNA sample in any assault case, the DNA results are entered into a nationwide database. Upon entering Mr. Gray's DNA into the database, it came back with four other hits. His DNA matched four other rape victims in the area.

According to court documents, Mr. Gray had been identified using a genetic marker taken from semen samples that were collected from the rape kits of each of his victims. None of the other victims were able to positively identify him except for me. The DNA match identified him as the rapist of all five victims.

Ms. Iqra was so thrilled. She knew this was the smoking gun she needed to win my case. At the time of his arrest, he had in his possession $50,000 worth of stolen checks from the public library. This case was going to be a slam dunk.

When I arrived at the DA's office, there was another young African American girl sitting in the waiting area. She looked to be in her early twenties—maybe twenty-one or twenty-two. Ms. Iqra came out to greet me and the young lady, and she called both of us into her office. I was a little dumbfounded. *What did she have to do with my case?* I thought. *Maybe she was the rapist's wife?* When we all sat down in Ms. Iqra's office, she introduced the young lady to me. Her name was Tamdeka Harrison. She was twenty years old, and she was also raped by Mr. Gray. Ms. Iqra asked if it was OK for us to have our meeting together because Tamdeka's encounter with Mr. Gray was very similar to mine.

Tamdeka told us her recollection of what happened to her. She had been waiting for a bus on Merrick Boulevard around ten o'clock one night, and a man pulled up to the bus stop. He rolled down the window to ask her something, but it was raining so hard that she couldn't hear him. She walked up to the window. She said at first, he just asked her basic questions, like what's your name, where are you going, things like that. She said she wasn't really paying attention to him, so she kind of brushed him off because she saw that the bus was coming a few blocks behind him.

When she went to turn around and walk back to the bus shelter, she thought he drove away because his rearview mirror hit her shoulder. The next thing she could remember was him hurling something over her head, grabbing her, and throwing her in the back of the truck. She didn't even hear him get out of the truck. She kicked and screamed, and he punched her, telling her to shut up as he drove around. He drove around for a few minutes. She didn't know where he was taking her, the same way he did with me, and he raped her right there in the truck.

While she told her story, my eyes filled with tears. My heart started thrashing, and I began to tremble. Ms. Iqra was right: our stories were very similar, and it scared me to think of how many more women there were out there that he had done this to.

The one major difference between my story and Tamdeka's story was that she really didn't get a good look at him, because it all happened so fast. All she saw was the truck and that he was a black male. She said he kept the blanket over her head the whole time. He looked away when she got out of the truck, so she never really saw his face.

As a result, the police were never able to make an arrest on her case—until now.

CHAPTER  11

Over the next few weeks, things began to progress rather quickly. After Ms. Iqra gathered the testimonies from each victim and presented them to the grand jury along with the DNA analysis, the rape kits from each of the five victims, and other evidence, he was perceived to be a serial rapist who attacked five women ranging in ages from seventeen to fifty-four from October 1996 to November 1997. The grand jury panel came back with an indictment of five counts of rape in the first degree, two counts of assault, three counts of kidnapping, multiple counts of sodomy, and theft.

Throughout the next few weeks, I had to go to Ms. Iqra's office a few more times to give my final deposition statement, go over my testimony, and prep for the trial. Her case was solid, and she was ready to proceed. She was so excited by the amount of DNA evidence. She was able to directly connect each one of the rapes to him and positively identify him as the rapist in each case.

I was still on the road to redemption. It was long and hard, and at times it didn't seem like there was any progress being made at all. But we had a date for the trial to begin, and I could finally tell my story, get closure, find peace, and move past this tragedy.

After three long years of waiting, the trial of The People of the State of New York against Frank Gray began on June 12, 2000. All five victims were prepped and ready to give their testimony to the most horrendous, brutal, and humiliating experience of our lives in a court of law in front of the man who had raped us.

Ms. Iqra had us testify in the order that we had been attacked, so that meant I would testify last. When you testify in a trial, you are not allowed to be in the courtroom until after you have given your testimony, so I was not able to sit in and listen to any of the other victims testify. I didn't even know what happened to the other ladies, except for Tamdeka.

After the trial, I was able to get a copy of the transcripts. That's when I read the testimonies of the other victims and realized the horror and turmoil they had to endure at the hands of our rapist.

According to these transcripts, the first victim, who was only seventeen at the time of her attack, testified that she was returning home from a party on the night of September 28, 1997. It was around three o'clock in the morning when a man in a jogging suit approached her near 114th Street and Liberty Avenue.

Starting out in a loud, clear voice and later breaking down in tears, she told the jury how Gray had stuck a gun in her ribs and ordered her into a garbage-filled alley, where he sexually assaulted her. This girl had a very small frame, but I could imagine that she sat tall and confident in the witness seat, speaking directly to the jury. "He told me he had a gun," she said. "I didn't see it; I felt it. He said to be quiet, or he'd kill me."

According to the young woman, Gray took her to an open garbage basement and raped her while she faced the wall. Coincidentally, this was just a few doors down from her home.

Mr. Gray's second and third victims testified later that day. A young Hispanic female in her mid-twenties took the stand next. She gave testimony that on October 8, 1996, while on her way to work at six o'clock in the morning, Gray had grabbed her and dragged into an alley and raped her. The next witness was an older white woman in her fifties. She told the court how Gray had approached her on April 13, 1997, punching her in the face several times. He grabbed her and dragged her to the back of a building and raped her. Hers was the most brutal of all the attacks.

Finally, when I read Tamdeka's testimony, I was even more shocked and shaken by this man's calculated and degrading actions. Tamdeka took the stand and testified that on a rainy night on August 21, 1997, her attacker threw a blanket over her head before he kidnapped her and then sexually assaulted her in his truck. She covered her face with her hands the entire time she testified. She never looked up at the jury, the defendant, or Ms. Iqra.

The trial lasted about three weeks. There was a lot of physical evidence. There were medical reports and testimony from experts regarding the DNA evidence. There was the timeline that had to be established, and each victim had to relive what happened to them in thoughtful detail. Each day I prayed for Ms. Iqra and the jury, I also prayed for the other victims as they sat in that witness chair and gave their testimonies.

Ms. Iqra told me she would put me on last because I was the last victim in the timeline. Also, my rape brought all the other cases together. It was finally my day to testify—June 24, 2000. The DA's office sent a car to pick us up. It was me, Lorraine, and Malik. They were both going to be called as witnesses.

I was so nervous, but there was an eerie calm about me. I was prepared to face my attacker and finally put all the anxiety, apprehension, and trauma behind me.

CHAPTER 12

It was a beautiful day outside. The sun was shining bright. I could feel the summer weather was finally here to stay. It was a great day for justice. We arrived at the courthouse around ten o'clock that morning. Ms. Iqra met us in the hallway and briefly went over the order in which we would testify. She told us that Malik would testify first, since he was the first person to see me when I walked through the door. Lorraine would go after me to confirm how the police were able to get Mr. Gray's phone number.

Malik was called to give testimony as to my emotional state when I came back to the house. He testified that I told him I was raped. Malik had a criminal past, which had no bearing whatsoever on my case. But the defense attorney, Daniel Masopovitch, took it as a chance to use my brother's past transgressions against him and destroy his trustworthiness. In a court of law, when an attorney can break down someone's credibility, it creates doubt and discredits that individual's testimony. Masopovitch asked, "What were you doing up at that hour?"

"I was selling drugs. You gotta stay up. Crackheads don't sleep," Malik said.

The jury laughed.

Masopovitch did not like that at all. He started asking him questions about his charges and his time in jail. He attempted to disgrace my brother's reliability by bringing up his past crimes. They called for my brother's criminal record.

The court took a break for lunch so the arrest records and court transcripts for my brother could be brought down to the courtroom. Meanwhile, Lorraine and I were standing in the hall, wondering what had happened. Ms. Iqra was confident that his testimony did not hurt our case and that it was just a ploy to get the jury's attention away from the defendant. In other words, the defense attorney was doing what he was paid to do: drive culpability away from the defendant by disregarding other people's statements and allegations. At this point, she felt that there was no need to have Lorraine testify, so she told me I would be up next.

The bailiff came out into the hallway to call me in. *This is it*, I thought to myself. *This is the day I become free*. I stood up and gave my brother and sister a hug and walked into the courtroom. My heart was beating so fast, and my legs were trembling a bit, but I kept my head held high. I looked straight ahead. The courtroom was a very intimidating place, especially when everyone else was facing you, including your attacker.

As I was sworn in, I heard some mumbling and snickering from the defendant's side of the courtroom, but I didn't look over there. I stood up straight,

I held up my right hand, and I swore that I would tell the truth and nothing but the truth, so help me God! I sat down quietly. I didn't look at anyone but the district attorney. She greeted me, then said, "I'm going to ask you some questions about what happened on the night of November 16, 1997."

Then she started walking toward a large board standing in the middle of the courtroom. There was a map of Queens County on the board with red pins in it, which I can only imagine were the locations of each of the five victims of this serial rapist.

The DA asked me the details of November 16, 1997—the night I was raped.

I told her the story the same way I had told it to the initial police officer, the detectives, the counselor, and the ADA herself.

The truth does not change. It stays consistent no matter how many times you tell the story. If it's the truth, it will not waver. As my father would say, "The truth is the truth is the truth." She asked me specific questions about going to the medical examiner's office to legitimize how the DNA evidence had been collected. She presented documents to support the chain of custody. Then she asked about the phone call to categorize how the police were able to contact the defendant. All in all, her case was solid, and she had all the evidence she needed to support the facts and get a guilty verdict.

The state had no further questions for me, and now it was the defendant's attorney's turn to cross-examine me. I was so nervous because I thought he was going to be all harsh and call me a hostile witness, but he didn't. Instead, he tried to assassinate my character in front of the judge and jury.

He went over my testimony again, trying to poke holes in it to get me to slip up. He asked me several times how I had met the defendant and if I had ever worked as a stripper. He asked if I was sure I had never met the defendant. Ms. Iqra stood up and shouted, "Objection!"

I was so humiliated and embarrassed. How was it possible for him to even be allowed to ask me those things? I mean, his client had raped *me* and four other women throughout that year, and he was going to ask me if I was a stripper! I was so furious that I was shaking. I was sweating, and I tried not to cry, but I was so angry that my eyes welled up with tears. I just looked down at my lap. I didn't even hear what he had asked me; then I heard Ms. Iqra object again, and the judge told the jury to disregard the last testimony.

I looked toward the jury box, and I saw a young white woman. She was probably in her early twenties. She looked at me as if she could see straight into my soul. I could see empathy and kindness in her eyes. I could tell she believed what I was saying and that she felt a great deal of empathy for me.

Mr. Masopovitch tried to disgrace my character by using my circumstances against me. I was a single mom, and I wasn't working. I was out late at night, but that didn't mean I asked to be raped. That didn't mean it was OK for his client to violate me or anyone else.

He tried to insinuate that I had to be a stripper or a prostitute and that the sex was consensual. You see, Mr. Gray was cocky enough to give his DNA because he believed he was only going to be charged with sexual misconduct. He didn't realize that DNA stays in the database until the statute of limitations runs out for that type of crime.

In the state of New York, there was no statute of limitation for rape. Had it not been for my quick thinking and giving him my sister's phone number, and had his wife not called me to catch what she thought was her husband cheating, none of the five victims would have gotten justice, and he would have gone on to continue to rape even more unsuspecting women. The judge asked the DA if she had any redirect for me. At that moment, Ms. Iqra stood up and said, "The state rests its case, Your Honor".

PART III

REDEMPTION

CHAPTER

It was finally coming to an end. From its inception, this case had been so unpredictable, so it was good that I was starting to find some closure. It was like I was letting go of the last bit of a heavy heart. Being a victim of such a vicious crime can put you in a very dark place—a place where as much as you are surrounded by people, you still feel unsettled, violated, and lonely. There is a popular saying that there is always a light at the end of the tunnel. I was finding my way out of the tunnel amidst all the obstacles in my way. I was finally getting the justice I deserved.

The defense began their case by calling their one and only witness to the stand: the defendant, Frank Gray. As I read the court transcripts, I learned that he had no defense whatsoever. He denied knowing any of the women except for me. His defense was that everyone was lying about him. He tried to convince the jury that knew me and that the sex was consensual. He told the jury that I was a prostitute. When I read that, I was so mortified and angry. But after watching so many court shows, I realized that his lawyer knew he would not be able to disprove any of the DNA evidence.

Of course, it would've been ideal for him to be able to explain how the defendant's DNA managed to get inside of me, but how does that explain how it was inside four other women at four different times in four different locations throughout Queens that year? His defense was weak. The trial ended the next day, and the judge retired the jury to deliberate until they reached a verdict.

Assistant District Attorney Miriam Iqra called over thirty witnesses over the three weeks of the trial. During her closing arguments, she stated, "The case against Gray hinges on three essential points: the tearful testimony of the five rape victims who described the attacks, the incriminating statements Gray made to the police after being arrested in June 1998, and the DNA evidence showing Gray had been in all five locations where the attacks took place." She felt my pain and the pain of the other four victims that suffered under the hands of Gray. Her statement reflected understanding, fairness, and facts. You could tell she wanted closure as well—closure based on justice. It felt good to have someone like her representing us. Unlike any other person, she fought hard to ensure that the court and jury could vividly imagine what we must have gone through. From an unbiased standpoint, I am yet to see such experience and competence as well as compassion in someone in the criminal justice system. I must say that the statement ran deep into the passions of the jury.

On June 29, 2000, the jury, which was predominately women, had found Frank Gray guilty of five counts of rape; five counts of sodomy; and two counts of kidnapping, sexual assault, and illegal possession of stolen checks. They unanimously decided that the defendant—who stood about six feet tall and weighed over 240 pounds—overpowered his victims from behind, dragged them into his vehicle, and then took them to a basement, an alley, or inside his truck and viciously sexually assaulted them.

All but one of his victims were in the courtroom the day the verdict was read. Tamdeka, the Indian girl, and I sat in one row; the young Hispanic girl sat in front of us. The older woman did not come back to court to hear the verdict. As difficult it was for me, I could not imagine how she was able to get through those last few years. She had a lot of physical injuries as well as emotional scars. I could only guess that she was happy to have finally faced her attacker in court, leaving the rest up to the criminal justice system.

As for me, I had to be there. Good, bad, or indifferent, I had to hear his fate.

After two days of deliberation, the jury had reached a verdict. When the jury foreman read the guilty verdict for each count of the indictment, and he said **GUILTY** on all counts, you could hear Gray's wife scream, "No!" Some of his other relatives were muttering in small protests about how the conviction was so wrong. The other three victims and I sat and held each other's hands and squeezed with joy. I had tears rolling down my face, and I just sat quietly and held my head down. My heart was overjoyed and relieved.

Judge Ronald Butner thanked the jury for their service and excused the jury. We all left the courtroom. The other three ladies cried and thanked me profusely. Each one of them, in their own way, told me that had I not been strong enough to tell what happened to me, none of them would have been able to get justice at all and this monster may have gone on to rape many more women. None of them were able to move forward with their case before and that I gave them the courage to move forward.

I didn't really know how to respond to that. I didn't think I was doing anything special. I certainly wasn't doing it for anyone else. All I knew was that somebody did something to me that I didn't ask for and it was not right, and that he needed to be punished for it. To be honest, I had to thank them as well. Had it not been for their cases being added on, my rape would have stopped at simple sexual misconduct, which was a misdemeanor, and he probably would have received a slap on the wrist for it.

In all actuality, we all needed each other in order to bring this vile man to justice. As much as I am a firm believer in karma, I also believe in making my own karma and getting justice for brutality. It felt good knowing that this serial rapist was going to jail for a very long time. It also felt good knowing that I was instrumental in helping to bring this dangerous serial rapist through the legal process.

It had been reported that the jurors said the case against Frank Gray was clear-cut because of the overwhelming scientific evidence against him.

One juror said, "In all honesty, the DNA evidence established the person. Then we looked at each count."

Another juror, who cried when the verdict was read, said, "The hard part was knowing that my decision put him away for the rest of his life." That statement was reported in a local newspaper.

As we exited the courthouse, a reporter from the newspaper came up to me and asked if I was willing to give her a story, and I agreed. My mind was still reeling in the fact that the man who raped me had just been found guilty after three years of waiting and wondering if he would ever be brought to trial. We went across the street to this diner and had lunch while she asked me questions about the trial and how I felt about the verdict. Honestly, at that moment, all I felt was deliverance. Later that week, I read her article in the newspaper, and that, too, gave me a great sense of pride and completion.

For privacy and security, rape victims' names are never listed in news publications, but reading the article I was able to point out some of the things I said to her and how she quoted what I expressed to her. The District Attorney himself stated, "The jury has declared the defendant a serial predator who sought out and raped five women. Were it not for DNA testing, these crimes might have never been solved." That alone made me feel as if the DA was thanking me personally. Reading that let me know that my tragedy had a purpose, and my anxiety and suffering was not in vain.

CHAPTER 14

July 14, 2000, was the day that this entire ordeal finally ended. It was the day the judge handed Mr. Gray the sentence for his crimes. Prior to reading the verdict, Ms. Iqra asked the judge if a few of the victims could read a statement.

Only three of us were there to hear the sentence. The young Indian girl—now twenty, then seventeen at the time of her rape—read her statement first. This girl had suffered the most. She was determined to somehow right this wrong. She was a baby when this happened to her. This man stole her innocence and her trust in humanity. She said, "I can no longer trust anybody. This attack has deteriorated my relationship with my father." She went on to say that she had trouble finding a job and often thought about suicide.

Tamdeka expressed how she had been an emotional mess for three years and experienced flashbacks and nightmares ever since her rape. She could never reclaim what had been taken away from her; neither of us could. Just by looking at her you could tell she had suffered a lot from the post-rape trauma.

There is something about rape that lives within you forever; it is a lot more than somebody snatching your bag and running off. It is more than having someone just hit you with their fist.

It goes along with what makes you normal—your self-esteem, social standing, and your dignity. People do not look at or experience you the same way anymore. It is even more painful when the perpetrator denies it and finds ways to go free while you suffer. Thanks to the DA's office and Ms. Iqra, this perpetrator was going to pay for his crimes.

I believe in justice. I also believe in natural laws and forces. The world is a funny place, where everyone gets a taste of their own medicine. We all pay for our sins before we leave this world. Gray's time was running out. He was on the verge of a major conviction. The justice system had descended on him. As much as that might sound vengeful, I believe he deserved some vengeance. The ordeals, as separate as they were, destroyed more than just five lives. The young Indian girl had a damaged relationship with her father, and the older woman could not even attend the hearing. We did not bring this upon ourselves; he brought this upon himself. In the process of hurting himself, he hurt all five of us, along with the suffering of our families.

The courtroom was silent. It was full of four of the five the victims; members of the police department; members of the press; members of the DA's office; several onlookers; and the defendant's friends, family, and his attorneys.

Before he read the sentence, Judge Butner commended the women for their courage and for coming forward and enduring the harshness of a trial. He told the defendant that no amount of time would be suitable for his heinous acts. He called him despicable and was glad that he would be off the streets.

Frank Gray received a sentence of 67½ to 140 years in prison. He received 12½ to 25 years for each rape, and the rest of the time was for the other charges to run consecutive, meaning that he must serve each term one after the other. In other words, he would spend the rest of his natural life in prison.

This time I didn't cry. I was tired of crying. This was a time to rejoice. I felt so proud and liberated. I felt like I was David, and I had just taken down Goliath. I won. The verdict gave me so much relief. He was never going to be able to hurt anyone else. As Mr. Gray was led out of the courtroom, you could hear his wife saying, "Pray. Just keep praying."

Later on, that night I did break down, and I cried because it was finally over. I felt delivered and free. I did it. I stood in front of my rapist, and I told the truth. My family believed me, the DA believed me, the judge believed me, and the jury believed me. I was finally vindicated.

I had been freed from the heavy shroud of shame, guilt, and blame. I imagined how the other victims felt about the ruling and if they felt the same way. I thanked God for giving me favor and working on my side. The next day I woke up and knew that something was different. The air felt different. My room looked different. I was different.

Rape is one the most underreported crimes in this country. Frank Gray was convicted of five counts of rape but imagine how many other women didn't even go to the police. Imagine how many more women he would have raped had I not gone to the police?

Approximately 25 percent of American women are victims of sexual abuse. Why don't we hear about it more? Why don't we talk about it more? Well, looking at the great amount of blame and judgment most rape victims face, and the limited amount of support and justice particularly African American women have historically received, it is no wonder that for so many women, especially *black* women, rape is a deep dark secret—a taboo subject never to be shared with anyone. Just as in the line from The Color Purple, said "you better not tell nobody but God!" For ages women have been taught not to tell.

As a society, we put so much shame on the victims of rape and sexual abuse crimes. We always hear, "She shouldn't have been out so late. She shouldn't have worn that. She shouldn't have gotten in that car. She shouldn't have been drinking." It's easier for us to believe that bad things happen to bad people or to someone who was doing something wrong.

That's why it's so hard for rape victims to come forward. You are automatically accused of participating in your own rape. Remaining anonymous as a victim of sexual assault is common. Black women are even less likely to report a rape than their white counterparts.

I, too, was going to be one of those women who didn't tell, but when I got back to my home, where I felt safe, I instantly found the courage and the strength to report it and to go through until the end.

The following week, I went to Ms. Iqra's office to officially thank her. I bought flowers and a card for her and a plaque to show her how much I appreciated all her hard work on the case. She was brought to tears when she read the card and told me there was no way she was giving up on my case. She told me she knew I was telling her the truth from the very beginning, because no matter how many times I had to repeat the story, I told it the same exact way. She said when people lie, they can't really remember small details or remain consistent when telling the same story over and over. She told me that this case was really hard for her, it took a toll on her emotionally and that this was her last case working in the sex crimes division. She would be moving on and leaving the Queens district attorney's office.

CHAPTER 15

Over the years I often thought about her and wondered how she was doing. Some years later, I read in the newspaper that she had gotten married and was working in the major crimes division in the Manhattan DA's office. Miriam Iqra restored my faith in humanity and the criminal justice system. She even restored my strength and faith in myself. She stood up for me and fought for me when I didn't think I had anyone, and she allowed me to finally find real closure and get the justice me and the other four women deserved after so many years of suffering.

All my life I have gone through trials, tribulations, and tragedy. Sometimes I feel as though I was born to struggle.

Surely my life has not been easy, but I also feel like God has a bigger purpose for me. This tragedy has led me to find my purpose. I have endured and overcome so many adversities in my life, and I truly believe that every single one of them has made me who I am today. Nothing is a coincidence. Everything that happens to us in life is meant to happen. It is either to teach you something about yourself or to bring you closer to finding your purpose. The road to redemption is never easy, but it is very necessary. My road was filled with many lumps and bumps along the way.

In 2002 my mother passed away from a stroke. She was a blessing to our family—a source of life and happiness for all of us. In fact, she was the pillar that held us all together. Soon after that, my sister moved out of the house, leaving me feeling alone yet again. It is true that time changes things. For me, time would begin to show me just how strong I really am. Right before my mother passed away, I had my second child. I knew life was not going to be the same, but this time I had two children to care for.

The one thing I have learned about myself is that I am extremely resilient. I have taken so many kicks and knocks, and I have been through so much, but I always managed to rise back up, dust myself off, and reinvent myself. A year after my mother's passing, I started a home day care business in her honor, which was very successful. I am now on the cusp of starting my own credit repair business as well as other business ventures creating health and beauty products.

Whereas Mr. Gray sits and rots in his prison cell, I am living free. I am starting businesses. I am falling in love. I am raising my children. I am finding my purpose and stepping into my destiny. I am becoming who God created me to be. I am finding out why I was expected to be so strong. The Bible says, "No weapon formed against you shall prosper" (Isaiah 54:17). It does not say they will not form;

it just says they will not prosper, and I am a living testament to that.

It has been twenty-three years since my rape. Over the last few years, I had a great epiphany: I realized that he didn't take anything from me. He didn't shame me in court; he didn't turn me into a victim. I had learned I was a survivor, and I always have been.

I didn't allow what happened to me to become me. Of course, it was very devastating at first, but I didn't allow it to totally consume my emotions and take control of my life. A lot of women never come back from being raped or physically assaulted, but I was one of the ones who did. I'm not special by any means. I don't have any superpowers. I'm just an ordinary girl from Queens who desired a normal life after a tragedy. I obviously did not ask for this tragedy to happen to me. In fact, it had never crossed my mind that I could ever be assaulted that way. Like any other person, I had trials and tribulations throughout my life, but I was determined to continue to do the best that I could for my son.

My life was not laid out perfectly for me. But with strength, determination, and willpower, even through many failures I was able to get back up every time I fell. I am proud today that I got back up stronger than ever. I was not ready to let all my life goals and aspirations fade into thin air because a man decided to violate and rape me. I am proud that I am living a life that I chose.

My road to redemption was not easy. Frankly, I'm still on it. I'm still making strides. I'm still falling down and getting back up. I am the same little black girl with the crooked smile; a loving, caring heart; and a generous soul with the strength and courage to bear the weight of the world on my shoulders while protecting and taking care of the ones I love. My road to redemption will come to an end when I truly find my purpose and fulfill my calling. Until then, I will remain true to myself, honor my parents, and take care of my children the best way that I know how.

When I think about the road ahead, I think of this excerpt from a Maya Angelou poem:

> *Out of the huts of history's shame, I rise.*
>
> *Up from a past that's rooted in pain, I rise.*
>
> *I'm a black ocean, leaping and wide,*
>
> *Welling and swelling I bear in the tide.*
>
> *Leaving behind nights of terror and fear,*
>
> *I rise.*

My triumph comes from my inner strength, and that's something I've always had. I'm not afraid anymore. I'm not ashamed anymore. After twenty-three years, I can walk outside without looking over my shoulder. The panic attacks went away, the nightmares have stopped and the anxiety is gone.

I can finally be proud of myself because I know I came through the worst thing that ever happened to me, and I won.

~The End~

Survivor Psalm
©Gifts from Within
I have been victimized.
I was in a fight that was
not a fair fight.
I did not ask for the fight.
I lost.
There is no shame in losing
such fights.
I have reached the stage of survivor and am no longer a
slave of victim status.
I look back with sadness rather than hate.
I look forward with hope
rather than despair.
I may never forget, but I need
not constantly remember.
I *was* a victim.
I *am* a survivor.

I am a survivor; that's all I know how to be.
I am not what happened to me. I am who I choose to become!

~Inshallah~

EPILOGUE

I have wanted to write this book for a very long time now. Very few people in my life even knew that this happened to me. I had never even told my firstborn son. I didn't really speak about my rape, because a part of me was still feeling the shame and guilt behind it. It was not until 2017, when the whole me too campaign came into the mainstream, and the whole world was talking about it and I didn't feel like I had to keep it to myself. I realized I was a part of that movement and that it was time for me to tell my story too.

Telling the truth about trauma is the only way to heal from it. I wrote this book to help women and young girls realize they can tell their story and find peace and closure. Whether the attacker is brought to justice or not, it can bring you so much gratification to know that you did what was right, and you don't have to be ashamed about it. The shame is not yours to bear. The guilt is not yours to hold.

You never know who your story will inspire. You are giving someone else hope when they're at a time when they think there is no hope. Sexual abuse in the African American community is also extremely taboo.

We are so used to being quiet and not saying anything for fear of breaking up the family or not getting anyone in trouble, but we must stop that. We have got to break that pathology in our culture. We have to teach our daughters and our sons to speak up if anyone sexually assaults or abuses them, whether it's your favorite cousin, favorite auntie or uncle, or even one of your parents or siblings.

Rape is a severely underreported crime in the United States, with surveys showing alarming statistics of up to 91.6 percent going unreported. Be the change you want to see in the world. Break the cycle; tell your story. It was not your fault!

REFERENCES

Bible Verse: http://www.lords-prayer-words.com/lord_traditional_king_james.html#ixzz54RBVZHzZ

Excerpt from *And, Still I Rise* by Maya Angelou. Copyright © 1978 by Maya Angelou. Reprinted by permission of Random House, Inc.

https://www.timesledger.com/stories/2000/27/20000706=archives35.html

https://www.timesledger.com/stories/2000/29/20000720=archives39.html

June 15: http://www.nydailynews.com/archives/news/defendant-id-rape-victim-linked-dna-5-attacks-article-1.864800

June 29: https://www.timesledger.com/stories/2000/26/20000629=archive39.html

June 30: http://www.nydailynews.com/archives/news/b-klyn-electrician-found-guilty-rape-spree-article-1.874275

July 15: http://www.nydailynews.com/archives/news/queens-rape-victims-broken-lives-article-1.885736

National Statistics: http://www.rrsonline.org/?page_id=944

Ochberg, Frank. "Frank Ochberg's 'Survivor Psalm'." *Gift from Within*, Joyce Boaz, 23 May 2015, www.giftfromwithin.org/html/Poetry-for-Trauma-and-PTSD-Survivors.html.

ABOUT THE AUTHOR

Lynda Vialet is a single mother with two sons. She spends most of her time working and providing for her family. She loves to cook; decorate; and host parties, barbeques, and events. She was born and raised in Jamaica, Queens, New York. She grew up in a household where her mother was a stay-at-home mom, and her father worked very hard to provide for and protect the family. She is the second oldest of four and the first girl, so she learned a lot of her nurturing and caring ways from watching her mom take care of not only her and her siblings but a majority of the entire family. Her mom was exclusively known as the family babysitter, so Lynda was raised among all her cousins and even some neighbors. She attended John Adams High School in Ozone Park, New York, and graduated at the age of seventeen with a regent's diploma.

Throughout her early career, she focused on the medical field, becoming a medical assistant and then a certified nursing assistant, as it was always her passion to help others. The tragic events depicted in this book, along with her passion, led her toward a career in the human services profession. While working a full-time job and being a full-time mother and grandmother, she decided to show her children that it's never too late to follow your dreams. In December 2017, she accomplished a longtime goal of earning her college degree. She graduated from Ashford University Online with a bachelor's degree in health and human services and a 3.36 GPA. She is an entrepreneur and now an accomplished author. She works as a tech support advisor while building a credit restoration agency. She currently resides in Atlanta, Georgia.